The Offi

FA

ENGLAND ANNUAL 1992

£4.50
UK ONLY

Contents

John Barnes playing in England's away (red) strip

Copyright © 1991 The Football Association Limited and Century 21 Merchandising Limited. Published in Great Britain by World International Publishing Ltd., An Egmont Company, Egmont House, PO Box 111, Great Ducie Street, Manchester M60 3BL.

Printed in Great Britain

ISBN 0 7498 0268 5

The Official FA England Annual has been written by David Barber, David Bloomfield and Glen Kirton of The Football Association.
Designed and typeset by Brian Folkard, edited by John Malam and picture research by Dick Wallis.

All pictures courtesy of Bob Thomas Sports Photography, with the exception of pages 8 and 9 (Action Images).

Cover photographs (top to bottom)
Gary Lineker; John Barnes; Paul Gascoigne; David Platt; Des Walker.

THE FOOTBALL ASSOCIATION

LIMITED

Founded 1863

Patron: HER MAJESTY THE QUEEN
President: H.R.H. THE DUKE OF KENT
Chairman: F. A. MILLICHIP

Chief Executive:
R. H. G. KELLY FCIS

Phone: 071-402 7151/071-262 4542
Telex: 261110
Facsimile: 071-402 0486

16 LANCASTER GATE, LONDON W2 3LW

Dear England Supporter,

Welcome to the third FA England Annual. Back in the 1950s and
'60s The Football Association put out a publication called 'The
FA Book for Boys' – it seems quite a remarkable title in the
1990s because today there is no reason why girls can't enjoy
football just as much as any boy. And now it is not uncommon to
see girls playing in school teams. To some people's eyes this
seems quite a revolutionary idea but perhaps, in 20 or so years,
we will wonder what the fuss was about!

    I think that this year we have managed to produce
the best FA England Annual yet – the articles are
interesting and informative,
and that was certainly the plan!

    If there is an issue that
you think we ought to have tackled,
I would be pleased to hear your
views and perhaps we could include
a few of your ideas next year.
Write to me at the above address.

    Enjoy your football – and
good luck with the Soccer
Knowledge quizzes.

Yours faithfully

GRAHAM TAYLOR
ENGLAND TEAM MANAGER

PS Don't forget to enter
this year's top prize
competition on page 58!

New Opponents for England

What do international teams from the Faroe Islands and San Marino have in common? Answer: they are both new opponents for England.

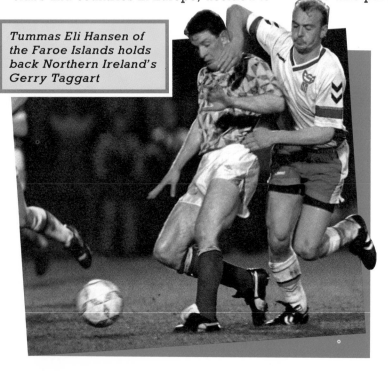

When England played Albania in the World Cup qualifying competition on 8 March 1989, the set of matches against European countries had been completed. England had played at least one match against everybody in Europe. Included in the list are games against two countries that no longer exist – Bohemia and East Germany!

But no sooner had that record been achieved, than two new opponents came on the scene. UEFA, which is the body that runs football in Europe and organises many competitions for clubs and countries in Europe, decided to allow the national teams of two tiny countries to take part in the European Championship.

Tummas Eli Hansen of the Faroe Islands holds back Northern Ireland's Gerry Taggart

The first of these was the Faroe Islands. Stuck half way between Iceland and the north of Scotland, the country consists of a group of 22 islands with people living on 18 of them. The population is only 46,000 and there are no grass football pitches. 22 teams play in the League and there are only 3,500 players altogether. The clubs rejoice in such exciting and romantic names as B71, K1 and H36! Because there are no grass pitches, UEFA ordered the Faroe Islands to play all of their matches in another country. They chose Sweden and played their first ever European Championship match against Austria on 12 September 1990. The whole world was astonished when the Faroes beat

May 1991 and the Faroe islanders celebrate their 1-1 draw with Northern Ireland

can do against the giants of world football. With at least six countries from the developing nations playing in the World Cup Finals these days, it isn't surprising that England are meeting new opponents all the time. The example that everybody will be able to think of straight away is, of course, Cameroon. Nobody who saw that fantastic World Cup quarter-final in Naples on 1 July 1990 will ever be able to forget how close the Africans came to reaching the semi-finals at England's expense. A Peter Shilton save away from being 3–1 down with ten minutes to go, England roared back to grab an equaliser with Gary Lineker's penalty, then went on to win in extra time. It had been a big scare.

Within the last ten years, England have also played first games against Iceland, Canada, Israel, Malaysia, Kuwait, Paraguay, Saudi Arabia, New Zealand and Turkey. Hardly any of the games have been walk-overs. As the years go by, more and more countries will emerge and England will surely travel across the world to meet many new footballing rivals and make new football friends.

Jan Dam of the Faroe Islands in action during the European Championship qualifier with Northern Ireland

the team that qualified for the 1990 World Cup by 1–0. The Faroes have come down to earth since in their other qualifying matches, but what a start for the fishermen of the North Atlantic.

The second team to have joined the European football family is San Marino. A tiny republic of 25,000 people totally surrounded by Italy, San Marino relies on tourists to earn a living. There is no National League and there are only 920 players registered with the 17 clubs. One or two of the best players are with Italian second and third division teams, but any sort of positive result against one of the bigger countries would be something of a miracle.

But it isn't just in the European Championship that England are making new friends on the football field. The increase in the number of countries qualifying for the World Cup Finals from 16 to 24 has given an opportunity to many Asian and African countries to show what they

England's Greatest Games

1963

England 2   Rest of the World 1

The Football Association came into being on 26 October 1863, when a meeting of members of the chief clubs and schools playing football decided to form an association for the purpose of framing a set of official rules under which all could play the game. This meeting was held at the Freemason's Tavern in London and a month later work on the law-making began. Those first rules may seem quaint today, but from them the game which is now played and enjoyed by millions has emerged and developed.

To mark the Centenary of The Football Association, a team to represent the Rest of the World was selected by FIFA (the game's world governing body) and met England at Wembley on 23 October 1963. The England squad and the 'World' team were presented to the Duke of Edinburgh and the Duke of Gloucester before the match.

England had opened their 1963–64 campaign in grand style with an easy 4–0 win in Wales. Relying on the same players (Gordon Banks, Bobby Moore, Jimmy Greaves and Bobby Charlton) who had performed so well on that summer's tour to Czechoslovakia (won 4–2), East Germany (won 2–1) and Switzerland (won 8–1), the side overwhelmed the Welsh defence in the latter stages of a one-sided game.

England took on the Rest of the World in their second match of the season and, playing with great determination, were full value for their 2–1 victory. FIFA had selected the following 'World' team: Yashin (USSR), Djalmar Santos (Brazil), Schnellinger (West Germany), Pluskal, Popluhar and Masopust (all Czechoslovakia), Kopa (France), Law (Scotland), Di Stefano (Spain), Eusebio (Portugal), Gento (Spain).

The five 'World' substitutes who came on during this showpiece match were: Soskic (Yugoslavia), Eyzaguirre (Chile), Baxter (Scotland), Seeler (West Germany) and Puskas (Spain).

England showed superior teamwork throughout the game and more than matched their famous opponents in both skill and tactics. The defence of Armfield, Wilson, Norman and Moore refused to be outwitted by the artistry of Alfredo Di Stefano, the brilliance of Denis Law, the lightning dashes of the Portuguese Eusebio and the cunning of Ferenc Puskas, the Hungarian 'Galloping Major' who

was then playing in Spain for Real Madrid.

In attack, Terry Paine gave Schnellinger a gruelling afternoon, while Greaves and Bobby Smith were ever alert for the chance to surprise, first Yashin and then Soskic in the 'World' goal. Gordon Milne and George Eastham, acting as midfield linkmen, worked in perfect harmony, while Charlton's grandstand finish paved the way to the winning goal in the closing minutes of the game. The capacity Wembley crowd certainly had plenty to applaud.

Shortly after half-time, Greaves finished off a 'mazy dribble' at speed by flicking the ball past Soskic, only to find that the referee had halted play to award a foul on Greaves himself on the edge of the penalty-area. But England were not to be deprived for long, and Paine scored the vital first goal in the 65th minute with a good shot, following a chipped centre by Smith from the left wing.

The elusive Scottish inside-forward, Law, one of the game's most entertaining personalities, slipped round Norman and Moore, seized on a through pass from Puskas and ran the ball round Banks before tapping home the equalizer on 83 minutes.

Only seven minutes remained but England were still able to conjure up a winning goal. A Charlton effort struck the post and Greaves hit the bar with Soskic well beaten. Then, with two minutes to go, Charlton swept by three defenders, forging his way goalwards, and had his shot parried by Soskic. Greaves, following up, promptly scored.

So it was a case of all's well that ends well – and The Football Association were left to look forward to the next 100 years. In the more immediate future, however, England faced Northern Ireland less than a month later in the first evening international match under lights at Wembley. A sparkling England won 8–3, and within three years Alf Ramsey's team were crowned world champions.

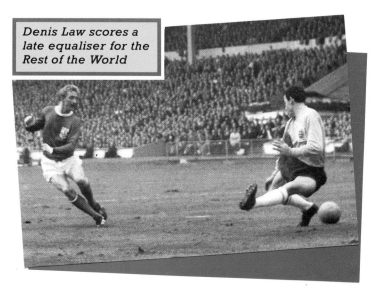

SOCCER
KNOWLEDGE
1

1
Who was the England Manager before Graham Taylor?

B.R.

2
If the Foxes were playing the Tigers, which two teams would you be watching?

3
Can a Third Division team win the FA Trophy?

YES

4
How many laws does the game of football have?

5
Which English team plays in the Scottish Football League?

6
Who plays at Griffin Park?

7
Bobby Robson left the England job to join which Dutch club?

P.S.V

8
What does 'Real' in Real Madrid stand for?

GREAT

9
If a club wins the FA Cup, what European Club competition do they qualify for?

CWC

10
Which Football League club plays in tangerine colours?

WOLVES

11
Which ex-international is the specialist goalkeeping coach to the England Squad?

G K

12
If the U's were at home to the O's in an FA Cup tie, which two teams would be playing?

13
Has Brian Clough ever managed Brighton and Hove Albion?

14
What was the 1990 World Cup mascot called?

P

15
Who is the Chief Executive of The Football Association?

Bobby Robson shakes hands with Peter Shilton who retired from international football

16

Can you be off-side from a throw-in?

NO

17

Which is the oldest Football League club? N C

18

If you were watching Groningen play Ajax, what country would you be in? H

19

Which outfield player has won the most caps for England?

BRC

20

Which company provides the footballs that England use in their internationals at Wembley?

M

21

Who did England play in Peter Shilton's last game for his country?

I

22

In international matches, are half-way line flags compulsory?

Y

23

True or False? Chris Waddle once had a job in a sausage factory.

T

24

Have England ever played Algeria in a full international?

Y

25

In football, what does the term 'nutmeg' mean?

Answers on page 61

England's Chris Waddle and West Germany's Rudi Voeller challenge for the ball

European Championship 1992

Stockholm's Rasunda Stadium – Sweden's most famous ground

The European Championship finals take place in June 1992 in Sweden, with the host nation joined by the seven group winners. This is not the first time that the Scandinavian country has hosted a big sporting occasion. The Olympic Games were held in Stockholm in 1912 and, of course, Sweden staged the 1958 World Cup, won by Brazil with 17-year-old Pelé making his debut on the world stage. Sweden's national team finished as runners-up to Brazil and have now become established as one of Europe's top teams. They will not start this summer as European favourites, but neither will they be a walk-over.

England's last three results in Sweden have been 0–0, 0–1, and 0–0, and as long ago as 1959 Sweden shocked everyone by becoming only the second overseas team to win at Wembley. Set against that must be England's great performance in the 1990 World Cup, compared with Sweden's three defeats in the same competition.

But the past will count for little when the tournament gets under way on 10 June. As usual, the eight competing countries will be divided into two mini-leagues of four. Group One will contain teams numbered 1 to 4 and the second group will have the countries 5 to 8. The winners of Group One will play the second team in Group Two in the first semi-final and the other semi-final will have the runners-up in Group One against the winners of Group Two.

Only four grounds will be used. The opening match will be in Solna, which is on the outskirts of Stockholm, at the Rasunda Stadium. The ground holds 40,400 spectators –

22,400 seated and 18,000 standing. Another two group games will be staged here, together with one of the semi-finals. The Rasunda is home ground to two Swedish First Division teams, AIK and Djurgårdens IF.

The other semi-final and the final itself will take place in the Ullevi Stadium in Gothenburg. This stadium holds 45,000 people, of whom 22,400 will have seats. The record attendance at this ground is 64,312 – but not for a football match. This massive crowd was attracted to a Bruce Springsteen concert in June 1985! Three Swedish First

THE FINALS

Date	Match	Venue	Time	Teams
10 June	1	Stockholm	20.15	1–2
11 June	2	Malmö	20.15	3–4
12 June	3	Gothenburg	17.15	5–6
12 June	4	Norrköping	20.15	7–8
14 June	5	Stockholm	20.15	1–3
14 June	6	Malmö	17.15	2–4
15 June	7	Gothenburg	20.15	5–7
15 June	8	Norrköping	17.15	6–8
17 June	9	Stockholm	20.15	1–4
17 June	10	Malmö	20.15	2–3
18 June	11	Gothenburg	20.15	5–8
18 June	12	Norrköping	20.15	6–7
Semi-finals				
21 June	13	Stockholm	20.15	Group 1:1–Group 2:2
22 June	14	Gothenburg	20.15	Group 2:1–Group 1:2
26 June	15	Gothenburg	20.15	Final

The eight finalists will be numbered by a new draw, made after the qualifying matches. Two places are reserved: Sweden will be team No.1 and Holland, as reigning champions, No.5 – provided Holland qualify for the finals. Otherwise the team ranked first in Europe at the time of the draw will be team No.5.

Division teams play here – GAIS, IFK Göteborg and Örgryte IS. The ground will also stage three of the group games.

The third ground to be used is Malmö Stadium, home of the former European Cup finalists, Malmö FF. The stadium has a capacity of 31,000, of which 16,000 are seats and 15,000 standing places. Three group games will be played at this ground.

The last ground to be used is Norrköping. Three group matches are due to be played here, in front of maximum crowds of 23,000 of whom 15,000 will be standing and 8,000 seated. Home club is IFK Norrköping.

Conditions should be perfect for football. June is right in the middle of the Swedish football season, with the weather traditionally warm, but not uncomfortably so, and the days stretching out to well past ten o'clock at night. It should be a great tournament for the fans and the players.

England Captains

England captains are born, not made, and it is the ambition of all who play for their country that one day they should lead it too.

There can be no greater honour in the game of football than to be chosen to captain your country. It is the pinnacle of any professional player's career. He has been recognised by the team manager as the best player in the land in one particular playing position and as having those special qualities of leadership, exemplary play and charisma that go together to make a natural team captain.

Certain players stay in the mind as great England captains – Billy Wright, Johnny Haynes, Bobby Moore, Kevin Keegan and Bryan Robson to name just a handful. Moore will perhaps remain the most famous of all, having received the Jules Rimet Trophy from HM The Queen on that historic July day in 1966. The brilliantly gifted West Ham defender had skippered the England Youth Team before he became England's youngest ever captain in 1963 at the age of 22, when the team won 4–2 in Czechoslovakia. Before that friendly match in Bratislava, Moore had only appeared in 11 full internationals. He captained England for the 50th time against Northern Ireland in Belfast in 1969 and for the 91st and last time in the Wembley friendly with Italy in 1973.

The best-known England captain of an earlier era was the Wolves defender, Billy Wright. He was first capped as 'right-half' against Belgium in 1946 (actually because another player had been forced to drop out) and after that missed only three of England's next 107 games – including a run of 46 consecutive games at centre-half. He captained the team under manager Walter Winterbottom on 90 occasions.

Wright's international career finished on a high note with England winning 8–1 against the USA in Los Angeles in 1959. At that time the England team contained some names which are still well-known today – Don Howe, Jimmy Greaves and Bobby Charlton for example. The England captain after Wright was the stylish Blackburn wing-half Ronnie Clayton. Then Johnny Haynes, who reputedly became the first £100-a-week professional

Bobby Moore, wearing the special England strip for 'The Football Association's centenary in 1963

Emlyn Hughes as captain in 1978, with Paddy Mulligan of the Republic of Ireland

Kevin Keegan in his days as England captain

Flowers filling in on a couple of occasions. Moore also led the team in the Mexico World Cup of 1970, turning in outstanding performances. Who could forget the picture of Moore embracing Pelé after that magnificent group match in Guadalajara in which his expertly-timed tackles had tamed Jairzinho?

After Moore and his mentor, Sir Alf Ramsey, had departed from the England scene, caretaker manager Joe Mercer turned to Emlyn Hughes for his captain. The hard-tackling Liverpool defender captained England in all the seven matches with Mercer in temporary command. Only one of those was lost. Then, under new boss Don Revie, Hughes gave way to Alan Ball who presided over two significant Wembley events – a 5–0 win over Cyprus (Malcolm MacDonald netted all five) and an even sweeter 5–1 victory against Scotland in the last game of the 1974–75 season.

footballer at Fulham, took over as skipper for 21 out of the next 22 games before giving way to Jimmy Armfield after the 1962 World Cup. England had been tremendously successful at the start of Haynes's period with the captain's armband. They won all the first six internationals of season 1960–61, when the results in England's favour were 5–2, 9–0, 4–2, 5–1, 9–3 and 8–0! Haynes, though noted more as a goal-provider than a goal-scorer, managed to grab four himself.

In the build-up to the next World Cup (in England), Moore skippered England in almost every game, with Wolves wing-half Ron

Bryan Robson exchanges gifts with Kevin Moran of the Republic of Ireland, March 1991

QPR midfielder Gerry Francis put on the armband for the first three matches of the following season and Kevin Keegan did so for the first time in the Football Association of Wales centenary fixture in Wrexham (England won 2–1). Keegan captained England on 31 occasions and Bobby Robson's man and namesake Bryan Robson was captain 65 times. England had three different skippers at Italia '90 – Robson, Shilton and Butcher – and it was super striker Gary Lineker who was afforded the ultimate football honour as England began the 1990–91 season under Graham Taylor.

Gary Lineker, England's new captain under Graham Taylor with his counterpart from Turkey, May 1991

Graham Taylor England Manager

He's the new manager of England, but what's he like, and what experience can he bring to the hardest job of them all?

When Bobby Robson joined PSV Eindhoven in Holland after Italia '90, The Football Association chose Graham Taylor to take up the reins as England manager. It is a high-profile job with every football supporter in the country having their own ideas as to who should be in the team!

Above: Graham Taylor
Left: Lawrie McMenemy at Bisham Abbey, England's training ground

Being manager of the international team is a very different job from managing a club side because the England team play around only ten matches a season. A top club will play over 50 games where you can gradually implement changes in the team and tactics. The England manager has less time with the players but Graham Taylor has always taken the view that whatever the situation you are faced with, you must try to work that bit harder and overcome the obstacles that are put in your way.

Graham Taylor was an obvious choice for the biggest job in English football after a managerial career in which one achievement followed another. In his playing days he was a full-back for Grimsby Town and Lincoln City and when aged only 20 had given indication of things to come when he became the youngest fully-qualified FA coach. A serious injury brought his career to an abrupt end but then at the age of only 28, he became the youngest manager in the Football League, at Lincoln City. In 1976 he led Lincoln to the Fourth Division Championship and was soon hand-picked by Watford who, now with financial backing of Elton John, were determined to make rapid progress in their status. The Fourth and Third Division titles were soon collected in consecutive seasons and after finishing runners-up in the Second Division in 1982, Watford were in the First Division for the first time in their history. The journey had taken just five years. The record books will tell you that Graham Taylor's main achievements at Vicarage Road were to take the club to a runners-up position in both the Football League Championship and in the FA Cup. But in addition to on-the-field success, there was plenty to admire elsewhere. He pioneered the concept of a club being actively involved in the local community. Amongst other innovations, players were expected to give freely of their time to pursue this aim by attending schools and giving coaching

sessions and Watford were among the first to open a family enclosure.

After ten years with Watford he joined Aston Villa, then of the Second Division. Under new management they immediately won promotion to the top flight and in his last season at Villa Park his team were runners-up to the mighty Liverpool. Then came the call from Lancaster Gate.

One of Graham Taylor's first decisions was to ask Lawrie McMenemy to join him in the role of Team Manager's Assistant. Lawrie is best known for his work at Southampton, where as manager he built several fine attacking, attractive sides, taking the club to an FA Cup Final victory over Manchester United in 1976. Together, Graham Taylor and Lawrie McMenemy carry the hopes of all England supporters. But armed with their knowledge, experience and ambition, and with the World Cup in 1994 as their prime target, it seems certain that exciting times are ahead.

Graham Taylor shouts instructions during the match against Turkey, May 1991

Penalty!

Penalties for England are few and far between, but when they come they can be the making of the match.

Gary Lineker scores from the spot against Cameroon, February 1991

Gary Lineker weaves his way through a packed Cameroonian defence in the 1990 World Cup quarter-final in the San Paolo stadium in Naples. England are just eight minutes away from ignominious defeat against the Italia '90 African surprise package. Lineker is in the box, going round the last green-shirted defender, when he is tripped and brought crashing to the turf. Mexican referee Codesal sprints over to the spot and points sternly down, using both arms. Penalty! There could have been few penalty-kicks in the chequered history of the English international team as crucial as Lineker's on that sultry Italian evening. At a stage in the tournament when most of the remaining teams seemed to be dreading the prospect of a penalty shoot-out – England themselves had been seconds away from such a fate when

West Germany's Bodo Illgner saves Stuart Pearce's penalty kick, July 1990

David Platt's spectacular volley beat the Belgians – Bobby Robson was able to reflect on the fact that his England teams had been awarded only two penalties in 92 starts. Those supporters with good memories could recall Phil Neal's successful spot-kick against Wales at Wembley in 1983 and Bryan Robson's three years later when his penalty helped the team to victory in Israel.

Now, somewhat perversely, Lineker was slotting home two penalties inside 20 minutes – both for fouls committed on himself – to win a match that put England into their first World Cup semi-final since 1966 and the first ever on foreign soil. Then, three days later on a night of high drama, England finally lost to their old World Cup adversaries, West Germany, in a penalty shoot-out after two hours of absorbing football in Turin. The 62,000 spectators in the Delle Alpi stadium and probably as many as 25 million television viewers at home in England (not counting a billion or so around the globe) held their breath as the semi-final protagonists prepared to take five penalty-kicks each, to decide who would meet

penalty-takers for England. Alf Ramsey, who won worldwide fame and a knighthood as England's World Cup-winning manager in 1966, won 32 caps as a player and scored with a penalty during England's historic 6–3 defeat against the 'Mighty Magyars' of Hungary in 1953. A month earlier his spot-kick in the dying minutes had helped England to a thrilling 4–4 draw against FIFA in a special match to mark the FA's 90th anniversary.

Ron Flowers, a wing-half with Wolverhampton Wanderers, netted twice from the spot during England's Chilean World Cup challenge in 1962 – against Hungary (lost 2–1) and Argentina (won 3–1). Ultra-cool Allan Clarke, then of Leeds United, scored the penalty that beat Czechoslovakia in the Mexican World Cup in 1970 and also the one that gave England hope as they battled against the Poles for a place in the 1974 finals. When England were in danger of missing out again in 1982, Kevin Keegan stepped up to drill home the spot-kick that clinched a memorable 3–1 victory in Hungary in one of the last qualifying group matches.

The penalty-kick was first introduced into the game by the Irish FA in the 1890–91 season. The Argentina v Mexico World Cup match in 1930 had five spot-kicks in normal time.

Argentina in the final. Lineker blasted home from England's first attempt, and the kicks from Peter Beardsley and Platt also beat Bodo Illgner in the German goal. But things looked bleak after Stuart Pearce's thunderbolt had cannoned to safety off the goalkeeper's legs. Then Chris Waddle's effort sailed over the top and England were out of the World Cup. West Germany's successful penalty-takers had been Brehme, Matthäus, Riedle and Thon, and they won the shoot-out 4–3.

So, during Bobby Robson's time as England's manager, his team had only been awarded four penalty kicks in 95 internationals (excluding shoot-outs). Under Graham Taylor, who succeeded Robson after Italia '90, the ratio was soon markedly different with two in his first four games. Lineker netted from the spot (after a handball offence) to give England the lead in their opening European Championship qualifier with Poland and was also on target with a penalty for a foul on himself against Cameroon.
Now let's have a look at some other

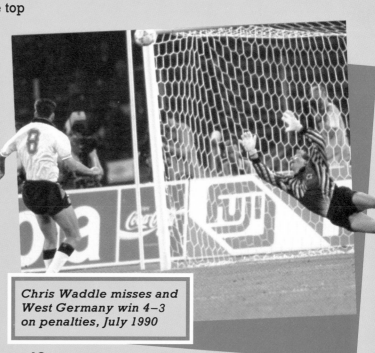

Chris Waddle misses and West Germany win 4–3 on penalties, July 1990

England's Greatest Games

1970

West Germany 3   England 2

By way of acclimatizing the team, Sir Alf Ramsey took his reigning world champions to defend their title in Mexico in May 1970, by way of playing two friendlies in Colombia (won 4–0) and Ecuador (won 2–0). He was convinced that his squad was actually stronger than it had been four years earlier when England had lifted the world crown.

His three undeniably world-class performers from 1966 – Gordon Banks, Bobby Moore and Bobby Charlton – were still there. So were Alan Ball, Martin Peters and hat-trick hero Geoff Hurst. Others who now contributed to a line-up good enough, so Ramsey thought, to retain the Jules Rimet Trophy were players of the quality of left full-back Terry Cooper from Don Revie's powerful Leeds United outfit, Norman 'Bites Your Legs' Hunter from the same club in central defence, hard-running midfielders Colin Bell and Alan Mullery and exciting strikers Francis Lee and FA Cup-winner Peter Osgood. But because the matches were played in the early afternoon to fit in with European television schedules, the debilitating Mexican heat and the high altitude would surely take their toll on Ramsey's charges.

England played out their three group matches in steamy Guadalajara, beating Romania and Czechoslovakia by the only goal and losing a classic confrontation with the eventual World Cup winners Brazil – a match mostly remembered for Banks's astonishing agility in dealing with Pelé's bullet header towards the

bottom corner of the goal. Ramsey's men then moved on to their Leon quarter-final and were eliminated from the tournament in a match which produced an incredible turn-about. Millions watching at home on television could hardly believe what they were witnessing. England's opponents on that hot day in June 1970 were again West Germany, the vanquished side from four years earlier. Still they had the elegant 'Kaiser' Franz Beckenbauer in midfield and pocket-sized dynamo Uwe Seeler in attack, one of Germany's most popular sportsmen who was playing in his fourth World Cup. Now they also had a scoring machine called Gerd 'Der Bomber' Müller.

For 70 minutes England were in complete control and, with goals by Mullery and Peters after 31 and 49 minutes, they seemed well on the way to a place in the semi-finals. England had looked a great team up until that point, dominating the pattern of the match and sweeping aside the challenge of a formidable German XI with positive, vigorous and skilful football. Surely they were home and dry at 2–0. Or were they?

England's Peter Bonetti walks off dejectedly after the match

far post. With the score 2–2 at 90 minutes and a punishing extra half-hour to come, it was almost a replay of the 1966 match.

This time it was the Germans who proved victorious. Two minutes into the second period, right-winger Jürgen Grabowski, a recent substitute for 'Stan' Libuda, sped past Cooper and centred for Johannes Löhr to head back across the face of the goal. 'Der Bomber' gave the exposed Bonetti no chance with a fierce close-range volley. England were out of the finals and it was to take them 12 years to get back. Bobby Charlton, whom Ramsey had controversially withdrawn, with England 2–1 ahead, to 'save his legs' for the semi-final, never wore an England shirt again.

Beckenbauer, whose role had been merely to shackle the England maestro, relished his new freedom and moved forward to help his team to a sensational victory. It was a tremendous blow to English football and the country was stunned.

In a way it was ironic that the Germans, again managed by the wily veteran Helmut Schoen, should overhaul a two-goal deficit since England, whose main strength during Ramsey's seven-year reign had undoubtedly been their defence, inexplicably failed in what for them should have been the quite simple task of defending this two-goal lead for just 20 minutes.

The 70th minute produced a Beckenbauer shot from the edge of the box which was misjudged by stand-in goalkeeper Peter Bonetti (Banks had gone down with a stomach ailment) and bounced under his dive and on into the far corner of the goal. Then, with only nine minutes of normal time remaining, Seeler back-headed a strange goal from near the byeline after Karl-Heinz Schnellinger had punished Brian Labone's mistake with a tantalizing cross beyond the

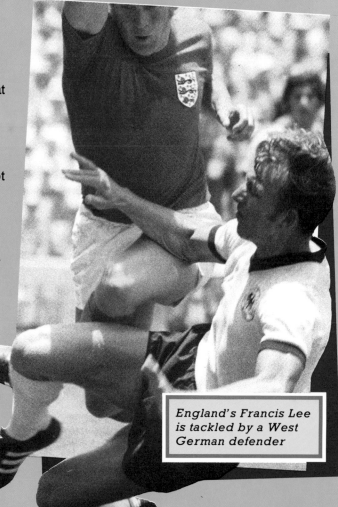

England's Francis Lee is tackled by a West German defender

SOCCER KNOWLEDGE 2

> *Paul Gascoigne tumbles to a West German foul, July 1990*

1
Which club did Graham Taylor manage before becoming the England boss?
A. *Watford*
B. *Aston Villa*
C. *Ipswich Town*

2
If you were watching a local derby at the San Siro Stadium, who would be playing?
A. *Stoke City v Port Vale*
B. *Roma v Lazio*
C. *AC Milan v Inter Milan*

3
Which club was runner-up in the First Division on three occasions in the 1980s?
A. *Nottingham Forest*
B. *Liverpool*
C. *Arsenal*

4
Which country has won more matches in the World Cup Finals than any other?
A. *England*
B. *Brazil*
C. *Italy*

5
Which was Stuart Pearce's first League club?
A. *Nottingham Forest*
B. *Coventry City*
C. *Port Vale*

6
Paul Gascoigne had a 'hit' with which song?
A. *World In Motion*
B. *I Should Be So Lucky*
C. *Fog On The Tyne*

7
Which club has as its theme song, 'Keep right on to the end of the road'?
A. *Preston North End*
B. *Birmingham City*
C. *Crewe Alexandra*

8
Which English team was the first to play in a European competition?
A. *London*
B. *Birmingham City*
C. *Manchester United*

Answers on page 61

9

Nigel Martyn was a £1m signing from which club?
A. Plymouth Argyle
B. Bristol City
C. Bristol Rovers

10

Which team is nicknamed 'The Wolves'?
A. Hull City
B. Wolverhampton Wanderers
C. Millwall

11

Which was the first African country to play at Wembley?
A. Cameroon
B. Morocco
C. Algeria

12

Who saved the first penalty in a Wembley FA Cup Final?
A. Dave Beasant
B. Gordon Banks
C. Peter Shilton

13

Only one post-war manager has led two separate clubs to the First Division title. Who?
A. Brian Clough
B. Bertie Mee
C. Ron Saunders

14

Who did Manchester United defeat 4–1 at Wembley in 1968 to win the European Cup?
A. Sheffield Wednesday
B. Benfica
C. Real Madrid

15

Where was Tony Dorigo born?
A. Birmingham
B. London
C. Melbourne

16

What is Gary Lineker's middle name?
A. Jason
B. Gavin
C. Winston

17

Who scored a hat-trick for England in the 1966 World Cup Final?
A. Bobby Charlton
B. Geoff Hurst
C. Jimmy Greaves

18

Lothar Matthäus is a driving force in midfield for which country?
A. Germany
B. Scotland
C. Holland

19

Which footballer is famous for refusing to appear on 'This is Your Life'?
A. Bobby Charlton
B. Jackie Charlton
C. Danny Blanchflower

20

Which team did both Rodney Marsh and George Best play for?
A. Manchester United
B. Fulham
C. Manchester City

21

Which country plays most of its internationals in Seville?
A. Spain
B. Portugal
C. Norway

22

How many goals did Kevin Keegan score for England?
A. 49
B. 21
C. 7

23

Which club released David Platt on a free transfer?
A. Manchester United
B. Aston Villa
C. Crystal Palace

24

Johann Cruyff played for and managed which Spanish team?
A. AC Milan
B. Real Madrid
C. Barcelona

25

Who is the England Team Manager's assistant?
A. Ray Harford
B. Andy Roxburgh
C. Lawrie McMenemy

David Platt celebrates after scoring the winner against Belgium, June 1990

The Manager's Job

How does Graham Taylor decide which team to field? How does he 'weigh up' the opposition?

"When England play an international match there is a great deal of work that needs to be done before the team can step on to the pitch. At least if we are playing at Wembley I know that the pitch is going to be in very good condition but when we play abroad, the situation is out of our hands.

Graham Taylor points the way during training for the match against Turkey

Walk this way... Graham Taylor leads training at Bisham Abbey

The night before an away match, I like to take the team to see the stadium. Although there will be no spectators around, it gives the players a chance to familiarise themselves with the ground and the pitch. This gives them an opportunity to see what boots and studs to wear as we usually have a short practice match session.

But our planning for a match does not begin the night before the game. Often months before the fixture, the FA travel manager, Brian Scott and my assistant Lawrie McMenemy, will go to the country we are playing and select a hotel and training ground for the team. Obviously the hotel needs to be able to provide privacy and good quality food and the training ground needs to have a good pitch and not be too far away from the hotel.

After each match, I call a meeting at Lancaster Gate which is attended by members of the FA staff. Lawrie, of course, is there, along with Glen Kirton (team administrator), David Bloomfield (press officer), Brian Scott, Adrian Titcombe (security) and Michelle Rogers (international secretary). Between us we

discuss how the arrangements went for the previous match and see if there is any room for improvement that we can introduce in time for the next match. We try to consider every issue, even to the extent of ensuring that the players can get home safely because we often land at the airport very late at night or early in the morning. Everything is geared to making the operation as smooth as possible and giving the team the best chance of winning.

If at all possible, I will try to watch the opposition in action. Also, I will try to get a few videos of them playing. Every team has its strengths and weaknesses and by watching closely I hope to spot these.

Perhaps they have a particular move that they like to use. It could be that one of their midfield players will like to run from a deep position, hoping to lose his marker if a long ball is put over our defence. I never worry too much about the opposition but it is better to know about a team's tricks than be caught unawares.

I also look for any signs of weakness. It could be that they have a central defender who is slow and we may try to create a position where he is in a one-to-one situation with one of our quick forwards.

I also have a handful of scouts who watch a lot of games for me and they will prepare a report for me to read. If it is a match in this country there will be one or two players who are on my mind to include in a Senior, 'B' or Under-21 squad. I like to keep up-to-date about a player's current form at club level but I always have to ask myself the question, '*How do I think he will fare at international level?*'

In the final analysis, a manager has to rely on his players. This is especially so with the England manager because although I may have many players to choose from, I can't buy one from another country and include him in my team. All a manager can do is to try to pick the right players and create the environment in which their abilities can come together into a winning team. **"**

Cap Centurians

Playing for England is one thing – to play for England 100 times is something else! Here are England's most-capped players – centurians at international level.

When Bryan Robson, England's captain, limped out of the 1990 World Cup group match against Holland in Cagliari, he was 13 appearances short of emulating four other England footballers who have each won 100 international caps. For two players with over 80 appearances to their name – Kenny Sansom (86) and Ray Wilkins (84) – it was fair to say that their England careers were probably over. But 'Captain Marvel' recovered from the injury sustained in Italia '90 and was back as England's skipper to face Cameroon in February 1991 and notch up his 88th cap.

The first 'centurian' for England was William Ambrose 'Billy' Wright CBE. He had begun his career at Wolverhampton Wanderers as a boy on the ground staff, and he remained with the club throughout his playing career, eventually proving to be an inspiring captain for both club and country. His 105 appearances in full internationals were made up of 51 games at right-half, 46 consecutive games at centre-half and eight at left-half. He captained England on 90 occasions (a world record) – the first time in the match against Ireland in 1948, when he took over from Frank Swift who had skippered the side in the previous two internationals.

Billy Wright's career finished on a high note as England thrashed the USA 8–1 in the last fixture of the 1958–59 season.

Bobby Charlton CBE joined Manchester United straight from school in 1953 and made his League debut against Charlton Athletic, scoring twice, three years later. He soon became famous for his powerful, accurate shooting, and was first capped at the age of 20 against Scotland, scoring one of the goals in England's emphatic 4–0 win at Hampden. He

Bobby Charlton and Bobby Moore – 214 caps between them, shown with Bulldog Bobby, England's 1982 World Cup mascot

was capped 106 times. He played in all the forward positions except outside-right and was one of the heroes of England's World Cup-winning team in 1966. One of football's greatest ambassadors, Charlton still holds the England scoring record with 49 goals (including four hat-tricks) and he overtook Billy Wright's caps total when he featured in that memorable World Cup quarter-final with West Germany in 1970. He was substituted, controversially, by Colin Bell and it turned out to be the great man's last England match.

Charlton's record was surpassed three years later by Bobby Moore OBE. Born in Barking, Essex, he joined West Ham United from school and quickly developed into a commanding wing-half and outstanding captain. He was skipper of the England Youth Team and made his senior appearance in Peru just before the World Cup finals of 1962. His twelfth full international appearance, in Czechoslovakia, was particularly significant because he became England's youngest ever captain at 22. Moore captained and inspired England to their wonderful World Cup triumph in 1966 and won the last of his 108 caps in the friendly against Italy in 1973. It was Sir Alf Ramsey's last Wembley match. 'Mooro' had scored just twice for England – against Poland and Norway early in 1966.

Peter Shilton MBE passed Moore's record when he was England's goalkeeper for the friendly in Denmark in 1989. The tremendously consistent Shilton had established a world record (for any position) with 125 caps by the time he announced his retirement from international

football at the end of Italia '90. He was first capped against East Germany in 1970 and would surely have amassed a much higher caps total had there not been the rivalry of Ray Clemence. The Liverpool goalkeeper had, for example, made 32 England appearances in a four-year period in the 1970s during which Shilton won a paltry three caps.

'Shilts' played under five different England managers and won caps whilst on the books of Leicester City, Stoke City, Nottingham Forest, Southampton and Derby County. He started all 16 England matches played in the 1989–90 season, conceding a mere 12 goals, and finished where he had always wanted to – at the top.

Left: Bryan Robson
Above: Peter Shilton receives an award from the FA in honour of his 100 England caps
Below: Bobby Charlton's cap century, 30 April 1970

England's Summer Tour 1991

June is not usually a month for soccer – at least not in England. But 'down under' soccer seasons are only just beginning and international games are possible. Graham Taylor's England side made the long trip and faced four games in 12 days on their 1991 summer tour.

Below: England's John Salako heads the ball
Bottom: Stuart Pearce of England is challenged by Australia's Alex Tobin

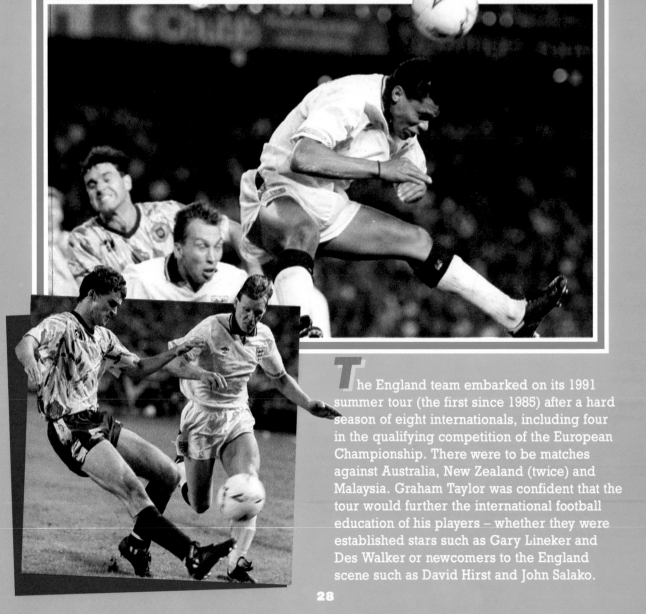

The England team embarked on its 1991 summer tour (the first since 1985) after a hard season of eight internationals, including four in the qualifying competition of the European Championship. There were to be matches against Australia, New Zealand (twice) and Malaysia. Graham Taylor was confident that the tour would further the international football education of his players – whether they were established stars such as Gary Lineker and Des Walker or newcomers to the England scene such as David Hirst and John Salako.

Australia v England

The Australian Soccer Federation was formed in 1961 and the 'Socceroos' qualified for the World Cup finals in 1974, finding themselves in a tough group that included East and West Germany. Ron Greenwood took an England senior side to Sydney for a one-off match in 1980 (won 2–1) and Bobby Robson took a senior squad over for a three-match tour in 1983 (won one, drew two). How would Graham Taylor's squad perform?

Right: England's Geoff Thomas plays the ball forward
Below: England's David Platt is held by Mehmet Durakovic of Australia

England's 1–0 win before a 35,000 crowd in the Sydney Football Stadium was a satisfactory start to the 1991 tour. The team had endured a 22-hour flight (with a time difference of nine hours at the end of it) and then had only a couple of days to recover before their match against the highly-motivated Australians. The match turned on a four-minute spell near half-time. Chris Woods reacted superbly to push away Gray's diving header from point-blank range and then the Aussie No. 2 scored an unlucky own goal as he attempted a clearance from Stuart Pearce's free-kick.

England's
Summer Tour
1991

New Zealand v England

The New Zealand Football Association was formed in 1891 and the two matches with Graham Taylor's England formed part of their centenary celebrations. The 'Kiwis' made it to the Spanish World Cup finals of 1982 and had gained priceless international experience against Brazil, the USSR and Scotland. England had never met New Zealand at senior level before, but a 'B' team had toured in 1978.

England's second match of the 1991 tour, played at Mount Smart Stadium in Auckland, resulted in another single-goal victory. But the tourists had to wait until the third minute of stoppage time for the clinching goal from Gary Lineker – his 41st for England.

The England skipper was missing from the next match, five days later at Athletic Park in Wellington, having flown to Japan to play for his club side, Tottenham. Stuart Pearce wore the captain's armband for the first time and scored with a firm left-footer on 12 minutes to give England a perfect start. The tourists handled the blustery conditions well and substitute David Hirst, in only his second appearance for England, netted five minutes into the second period to make the final score 2–0 on the ground which is the spiritual home of the famous New Zealand 'All Blacks' rugby team.

Above: Dennis Wise of England
Below: England's David Batty moves away from New Zealand's Robert Ironside

30

Malaysia v England

The Football Association of Malaysia was formed in 1933 and the national team has never reached the World Cup finals, though it *has* participated in the Olympic finals. Bobby Robson had taken an England 'B' team to Malaysia in 1978 (drew 1–1) but the two countries had never met at senior level. A capacity crowd of 45,000 in Kuala Lumpur's Merdeka Stadium sweltered in the humidity as Gary Lineker notched all four goals in a 4–2 victory for England, including a hat-trick in the first half. He thereby overtook Jimmy Greaves's England total (44) to come within four of Bobby Charlton's all-time England record (49).

In Graham Taylor's debut season as England manager, the team had remained undefeated in the 12 internationals played. A weary England party arrived back in London after a 15-hour flight for a well-earned rest. In little more than a month's time they would be reporting back to their League clubs for pre-season training!

Above: New Zealand's Declan Edge crosses the ball past England's Earl Barrett
Below: Gary Lineker scores England's goal in the 90th minute against New Zealand at Auckland

P	W	D	L	F	A
4	4	0	0	8	2

Lineker 5; Hirst 1; Pearce 1; own goal 1

31

England's Greatest Games

1981

England 1 Hungary 0

English international football was in the doldrums in the 1970s. After England lost their epic World Cup quarter-final with West Germany in 1970 (see page 20) it was to be another 12 years before they took their place on the world stage again – in the Spanish finals of 1982. England were absent in 1974, after Poland had gained the 1–1 draw at Wembley which saw them qualify for the finals at England's expense, and also in 1978 when Italy's superior goal difference in the qualifying group booked their trip to Argentina.

England finally made it to the World Cup finals in 1982. But it was a rocky road to Spain, along which they were condemned, reprieved,

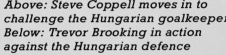

Above: Steve Coppell moves in to challenge the Hungarian goalkeeper
Below: Trevor Brooking in action against the Hungarian defence

condemned, reprieved again and finally let off the hook with a convincing win against Group Four winners Hungary in front of a 92,000 crowd at Wembley. The lowest point in England's fortunes had arrived in Basle as the team lost to Switzerland for the first time since 1947. Now they had accumulated a meagre five points from five qualifying matches and Ron Greenwood, England's manager for the past four years, was on the point of resigning. There was another disastrous defeat to come – against the plucky Norwegians in Oslo – but an impressive 3–1 win over Hungary in Budapest and Switzerland's completely unexpected victory in Bucharest gave England the opportunity to qualify 'by the back door'.

Needing just a point to qualify for Spain, England took both with relative ease on a cold November night, ending the months of nail-biting anxiety. Captain Kevin Keegan had stressed the need for patience in working for the vital opening goal but, as it happened, the important breakthrough came after only 16 minutes. Keegan had already headed straight at Meszaros (Hungary's giant goalkeeper with the thick black moustache) from a position almost identical to the one from which he had headed England's opening goal in a World Cup match of equal importance against Italy in 1977. But fortunately the miss did not prove costly for long.

West Ham's Alvin Martin, stepping into the team to replace the out-of-form Dave Watson at centre-half, challenged for a Terry McDermott cross. The ball fell to Trevor Brooking in acres of space and, even though the Hammers' midfielder's shot was weak and poorly directed, it was totally effective. At the far post Paul Mariner was on hand to divert the ball into the Hungarian net, probably with his shin. That, in truth, was the end of the match as a legitimate contest. Hungary's passage to the finals had already been booked and they were never a serious threat to Peter Shilton in England's goal.

Meanwhile, at the other end, England put together a series of scoring chances that were either missed or capably dealt with by Sporting Lisbon star Meszaros. McDermott lashed one volley just over the bar, while Mariner might well have had a hat-trick with a little more composure in front of goal. One header in particular, directed wide of an empty net, left the Ipswich striker shaking his head in disbelief.

A nasty knee injury to Steve Coppell, one that was to cause him problems later in his career and led to his substitution on the night, gave Ron Greenwood the opportunity to introduce

Paul Mariner is foiled by the goalkeeper

Tony Morley for his first taste of international football. The flying Villa winger looked to have done enough to suggest that he would be an essential ingredient in England's World Cup recipe. Only a spectacular save from Meszaros just before the end denied Morley a debut goal to savour. (He did, in fact, start the next two internationals but failed to make the squad for the finals.)

At the final whistle the jubilant England team acknowledged the tremendous support they had received from the capacity Wembley crowd. A lot could happen before Spain in seven months' time but, for the moment, the cry of 'England are back!' said it all.

1–0. Paul Mariner scores the only goal of the match

SOCCER KNOWLEDGE

3

1
In 1888–89 which team won the first ever League Championship?

2
Who wore the No.5 shirt when England won the World Cup in 1966?

3
Which club's supporters sang the Eton Boat Song at Wembley when their team won the 1987 FA Cup Final?

4
What is the full title of the FA Cup competition?

5
How many over-age players can play in an Under-21 team?

6
Valladolid, Logrones, Burgos, Real Betis and Valencia are all clubs from which country?

7
What gives a club the right to wear the Italian national flag on their shirts in the Italian Serie A?

8
They were a sensation in the 1990 World Cup, but who are the 'Indomitable Lions'?

9
Why are Plymouth Argyle nicknamed the Pilgrims?

10
Which two clubs did Kenny Dalglish play for?

11
In which country was the goalkeeper Ludek Miklosko born?

12
Which League club has played home matches on the most grounds?

13
In a League match, if the referee is injured, which of the two linesmen would take over?

14
Must players wear football boots and shin-pads?

Steve Bull is just beaten by the Dutch goalkeeper, June 1990

15

Who was England's leading goal-scorer in the 1990 World Cup Finals?

16

Which team are called the Foxes and play at Filbert Street?

17

True or false? David Platt played 134 League matches for Crewe Alexandra.

18

Nice, Caen, Cannes, Lyon and Nantes are all clubs from which country?

19

Who can be found playing home games at the Baseball Ground?

20

True or false? Bruce Grobbelaar played 24 League matches for Crewe Alexandra.

21

Which team lost the 1990 FA Cup Final but returned to Wembley a year later to win the ZDS Cup?

Answers on page 61

22

Which team is the older, Liverpool or Everton?

23

Which team is the older, Arsenal or Spurs?

24

Which team is the older, Manchester United or Manchester City?

25

Why does the famous Italian team Juventus wear black and white stripes?

Congratulations for David Platt after his goal against Belgium, June 1990

World Cup
USA 1994

You might not have heard of the Citrus Bowl or the Arrowhead Stadium – but when the 1994 World Cup comes around these are just two of the grounds in America that we will be hearing a lot about.

When FIFA, the world governing body of football, chose the USA to host the 1994 World Cup finals, many eyebrows were raised. The USA has never been a hot-bed for football, their sporting heroes have always come from grid-iron football, basketball or baseball. The country is also without a national professional league and the international team are considered to be something of a soft touch. So why did FIFA make this decision? Have they taken leave of their senses or have they made a wise choice?

The big attendances at the Olympic football tournament held in Los Angeles in 1984 gave the first indication to American soccer lovers

Above: Paul Caligiuri, USA
Left: Orange Bowl Stadium, Miami

that they could put together a serious bid to host the World Cup. Many people were surprised to discover the true level of popularity of a sport that they had long-regarded as something alien to the American public. Football proved to be more popular than athletics and from that moment on, it was clear that if the public were approached in the right way, there was a great deal of interest in the 'alien' game which for years had been ignored.

Most people watch the World Cup on TV rather than being at the actual matches, but imagine how embarrassing it would be for FIFA if the Final of the World Cup had over a billion TV viewers but only a handful of spectators in the ground. In England there are 3 million people who play football but in the USA they have 15 million who play regularly. Most of these players are youngsters but even if they can only produce one top player in a million, they should still be able to select an all-star team.

FIFA received serious bids from two other nations, Brazil and Morocco. Brazil has terrible economic problems and the country's resources are probably better spent on addressing social ills. One day the World Cup will be hosted by an African country but as yet they do not have the stadia to put together a serious bid.

One thing America has is stadia: grounds that put even the magnificent venues for Italia '90 in the shade. Many of them, however, do have artificial pitches, which will have to be replaced for the Finals themselves, as FIFA insist that World Cup matches can only be played on grass.

Being the host does have certain advantages in that the USA *will* automatically qualify and not have to face the rigours of qualifying matches. This is perhaps just as well, because when they defeated Trinidad and Tobago in November 1989 by 1–0, they qualified for Italia '90, and it was the first time they had appeared in the Finals for 40 years.

One problem that the organisers face is to convince the journalists and TV presenters that football is worth giving coverage to. They are so set in their ways, happy with the sports they know, that so far they have shown a reluctance to get behind soccer.

One of the aims of FIFA will be for the World Cup to raise the importance of football in American minds. The sport might have many players at junior level but the coverage in the newspapers it receives, compared to home-grown sports, is minimal.

One player who is helping the American cause is Sheffield Wednesday's John Hawkes. At home either as a full-back or in midfield, he has made a big impression and has already scored with a 40-yard shot against Peter Shilton. His progress is being followed by some sections of the American press and the youngsters playing there need examples to look up to.

Very soon the excitement of the World Cup will be here again. On 4 December 1993, the draw for the Finals will be made. Suddenly, stadia such as the Citrus Bowl in Florida, the Cotton Bowl in Dallas, and the Arrowhead Stadium in Missouri, will become very well known!

Peter Vermes, USA, in action against Trinidad, November 1989

Soccer's Emerging Nations

The game of international soccer is full of surprises. Cameroon was the surprise team of the 1990 World Cup finals – but who else should England watch out for?

At 10.32pm local time on Sunday, 1 July 1990, England were just a few minutes away from losing one of the most sensational quarter-finals in World Cup history. Gary Lineker's late penalty equaliser and his extra-time repeat finally saw England through, but opponents Cameroon were able to go home to Africa to a heroes' welcome. They had beaten the reigning champions, Argentina, become the first African country to reach the last eight, and excited fans all over the world with their open and attacking style of play.

Cameroon's Thomas N'Kono foils England's Gary Lineker

Ronald Gonzales of Costa Rica

But nobody should really have been surprised, because Cameroon were the last and most successful of a long line of African and Asian countries which had upset the 'big boys' of Europe and South America in every World Cup since 1966. Everybody remembers 1966 for England's great victory over West Germany in the Final, but just as remarkable at the time was the performance of little-fancied North Korea. The Koreans won through to the last eight by coming second in their first round group, beating mighty Italy 1–0 at Ayresome Park on the way. In the quarter-finals they met Portugal for a dream tie against favourites England and they made a brilliant start, rushing to a 3–0 lead after only 22 minutes. However, it didn't last long. Portugal's great striker, Eusebio, took hold of the game and his side finally ran out 5–3 winners.

There followed good performances in 1970 from Morocco, in 1974 from Australia and in 1978 from Iran when they ruined Scotland's hopes of progressing to the second phase with a 1–1 draw in Cordoba. The Spanish World Cup of 1982 saw even bigger strides by soccer's emerging nations. Algeria overcame West Germany 2–1 and were only denied a place in the next round when Germany and Austria played out a tame 0–0 draw to enable them both to go through. Cameroon, hinting at greater things to come, were just as unlucky. They held eventual champions Italy to a draw in the first round, drew their other two games in the group, but still failed to qualify for the next round. Along with Italy – and England – Cameroon could rightly claim that they had gone home undefeated.

Cameroon's good work was taken up in the Mexico finals of 1986 by Morocco. Drawn in the same group as England, Portugal and Poland, no one gave them much chance. But playing an attractive brand of football under their Brazilian coach, they held Poland to a 0–0 draw, then did the same against an anxious England. Bobby Robson's men, down to ten after Ray Wilkins had been sent off for throwing the ball down, could have been in real trouble if the Moroccans had shown a little more adventure.

Lots of attempts have been made to establish soccer in a country where grid-iron football, baseball and basketball are infinitely more popular. Association Football is being played in America by more and more people – there are some six million adult players, of which two million are female – but a successful professional league has proved very difficult to make popular.

Ahmed Ramzi of Egypt clears the ball from England's Steve Bull, June 1990

But 1990 was the year that finally saw the 'little' teams of world football come of age. Cameroon beat defending champions Argentina 1–0, talented Romania 2–1, Colombia 2–1 and then proceeded to scare England to death. The Central Americans, Costa Rica, appearing in their first finals, defeated Scotland and Sweden and made it into the last 16. Egypt finished all square with Holland and the Republic of Ireland and were only narrowly beaten by England (1–0) to be deprived of a place in the knock-out rounds. Only the United Arab Emirates and the United States seemed out of their depth, and yet even the Americans restricted Italy to a 1–0 scoreline and went very close to an equaliser.

The Americans will no doubt run an efficient and exciting tournament in 1994, but their performance in the tournament will probably decide whether America becomes one of the 'leading' soccer nations instead of one of the 'emerging' ones. FIFA, football's world governing body and the organisers of the World Cup, has determined that three countries from the African continent will qualify for the 1994 finals, so those 'big boys' of Europe and South America had better watch out. Nobody can say who will be the surprise teams of 1994 or of the World Cups to come after that. One thing is certain – surprises there will be and none of us should be surprised by that!

Tactics

Managers and coaches are constantly working for better ways in which to use their players. How important are tactics to England?

Above: Stuart Pearce with the Republic of Ireland's Dennis Irwin, March 1991
Below: Lee Dixon

Goals are scored by players, not tactics. But if a team has the right strategy, they give themselves the best chance of victory. A manager asks players to play in certain positions because he thinks it will be in the best interests of the team and he selects a formation that he feels will suit the players he has at his disposal.

Some of the very earliest games of football were between two villages with the goals often three or four miles apart from each other! The winning team was the one that forced the ball over the goal-line using any method they liked. It was an extremely rough sport, involving hundreds of men – and many legs and arms would be broken during the game. There were no tactics, just brute strength!

At least today, we know exactly how many players there are going to be on the pitch. But over the years, their positions and responsibilities have changed.

In 1966, England won the World Cup with a team managed by Alf Ramsey, later to become 'Sir Alf'. His side were called the 'wingless wonders'. This was because his team did not include a player who hogged the touchline. Most sides at this time featured two wingers. The England team did have wide players but they were expected to make a defensive contribution as well. This was a change in thinking and many teams, still to this day, play in the style made so famous by Sir Alf Ramsey. A more attacking version would be 4–3–3. You have the advantage of playing another forward but you have lost one of your midfield players.

Mark Wright scores England's goal against Egypt in the 1990 World Cup Finals

A feature of play on the Continent for some years has been the use of a sweeper. Very few English club sides have introduced this tactic but Bobby Robson did have some success with it in Italia '90. The sweeper is someone who plays behind the defence and if the opposing team's forwards get past the defence he is there to come in and prevent their move developing. He does not have the task of marking someone in particular – he is there to rescue the situation with a timely interception.

Because of this freedom the sweeper is often seen taking the ball out of defence into attacking areas of the pitch. Mark Wright was asked to perform this role and he emerged from the 1990 World Cup with great credit. Because a team has the extra security of a sweeper the full-backs are often allowed a more attacking role. They help the midfield players and get in as many crosses as possible. Stuart Pearce is one of the best examples of this tactic and he is often seen in advanced positions making an attacking contribution.

In some of the early games under Graham Taylor, England adopted a very positive approach by using only three full-time defenders with the full-backs, Lee Dixon and Stuart Pearce, playing so far forward that they could almost be classed as midfield players. In this situation the three midfield players suddenly have two of their colleagues lending their support. If the ball is in this area you might have five players and they will probably outnumber the opposition and hopefully be able to mount a successful attack.

The full-backs are a key ingredient in today's football. When the opposition is on the attack, they revert to a defensive role and now the team has five defenders (plus the goal-keeper). Again, hopefully, this is enough to repel any attack.

Wembley on Match Day

Football is a 90-minute game. Or is it? The game might be over quickly, but take a look behind the scenes to find out what else happens before an international game.

Centre stage at all of England's internationals at Wembley are, of course, the players. They are the people that the fans come to see, and it is their talent that sends the crowd home, more often than not, in a happy frame of mind. But no game could take place without the hard work and skill of a whole army of people beavering away behind the scenes on behalf of The Football Association and Wembley Stadium Ltd. The services that are there to make the match a more comfortable and enjoyable occasion for the fans don't just appear by magic. Long before the kick-off the people who sell food and drink to the supporters are working to get their booths and kiosks ready, bringing in barrels of refreshments, getting cooking equipment and food ready, counting change and putting it in tills.

Then there is the official match programme. This is produced by Wembley Stadium Ltd under the direction of the Programmes' Editor, Don Aldridge. The contents are passed to the FA where David Barber, one of the writers of this annual, checks them to make sure the facts are right. David Bloomfield, the FA's Press Officer and another contributor to this annual, writes the players' pen pictures. When everybody is happy, the programme goes away for printing and is subsequently delivered to Wembley Stadium, where hundreds of sellers try to make sure that everybody who comes to a match is able to get hold of a copy. As many as 50,000 might be sold at a big international, but for the FA Cup Final nearly 200,000 are printed, and bought in shops as well as by those actually going to the match. A hundred or so are taken to the dressing rooms as souvenirs for the players, the referee and the linesmen.

Wembley also run a shop and many kiosks that sell official England merchandise to the supporters. There are a lot of 'pirates' around the ground who sell poor copies of England scarves and similar items, so fans are advised to buy programmes and merchandise only at the official selling points. Stewards, who wear very distinctive uniforms, help fans to find their way and also sort out any problems that may arise. Then, of course, there are dozens

Wembley Stadium, London, England's home and one of the world's top grounds

watches a match from the Family Enclosure goes away with a souvenir of his or her visit as well as happy memories of the game.

An England international at Wembley calls for a great deal of preparation and planning. The sale of tickets has to be organised, the programme of events decided, special guests have to be invited and these sometimes include members of the Royal Family or top politicians. On the night, the VIPs and top FA officials have to be looked after, the Chief Guest has the teams presented to him or her on the pitch; if there is a match sponsor, that company's representatives have to be made to feel welcome and if there is a trophy to be presented, that has to be brought to the Royal Box at the right time. Responsible for all these tricky arrangements is the FA's Patricia Smith.

Then there is TV, Radio and the Press. Every England match is covered by more than 100 newspaper reporters, 50 photographers, at least two radio stations and on live television by BSkyB and recorded by BBC. David Bloomfield looks after the journalists in the Press Box, while Glen Kirton makes sure that there is always someone to act as a link between the TV people and the England team itself.

of policemen who ensure the safety of the public and without whom it would not be possible to stage any football matches. One special duty that the police have is to escort the two teams' motor coaches from their hotels and make sure that they arrive in good time at the stadium. The visiting national team usually stay in the West End of London, although when England played Poland in October 1990, the visitors decided to stay at the Wembley Hilton Hotel. They drove to the dressing rooms but could just as easily have walked! Another very important area at Wembley nowadays is the Family Enclosure. The Football Association is keen to encourage mums and dads to come to England internationals with their children and, with Wembley Stadium, they are working hard to make the Family Area a special place. The FA likes to ensure that every youngster who

Once players have arrived at the stadium many go straight on to the pitch to get a feel of the atmosphere and decide what studs to use. Most then leave tickets for friends and relatives before getting changed and beginning their warm-ups. As kick-off time draws near, the ball-boys, usually young players from one of the County Associations, take their places under the direction of Michael Appleby from the FA. Adrian Titcombe, a senior FA official, asks the teams to leave their dressing rooms. The referee and linesmen, accompanied by FA Referees' Secretary Colin Downey and an interpreter if necessary, come down to the Players' Tunnel from their dressing room and then Mr Titcombe leads the teams and match officials out on to the field for the pre-match presentations. Then we get down to the serious stuff!

England's Greatest Games

1987

Spain 2   England 4

In 1929, Spain had inflicted on England their first ever defeat in an international match on the continent, winning 4–3 in Madrid, and it was the Spaniards who provided tough opposition for Bobby Robson's team in the opening fixture of 1987 – on 18 February. England had begun the season with a single-goal reversal in Sweden – coming down to earth with the proverbial bump after the heady excitment of the 1986 Mexican World Cup – but subsequent European Championship victories against Northern Ireland (3-0) and Yugoslavia (2–0) at Wembley had given the team a much-needed lift.

Barcelona striker Gary Lineker had already registered two international hat-tricks – against Turkey and Poland – and went one better as England had a goal-crazy night in a remarkable Friendly at the Bernabeu Stadium. In his adopted homeland, England's six-goal hero of the '86 World Cup notched all four goals in a 4–2 win to bring his personal haul to 18 in 21 matches, an incredible scoring ratio.

But the defeat of Spain, their first at home for three years, was not in the least a one-man show. Peter Beardsley and Glenn Hoddle were at their creative best, Arsenal's Tony Adams had a confident debut in defence and collectively England were often inspired against one of the strongest footballing nations in Europe. There was an interesting statistic concerning 20-year-old Adams: he had become the first England player born *since* the 1966 World Cup to make his England senior debut.

England made such a promising start that they could easily have been 3–0 in front before Spain took a 14th-minute lead against the run of play. Emilio Butragueno, the Real Madrid striker (known as 'The Vulture') who a few months earlier had joined that select band of players to have scored four goals in a World Cup finals match, released team-mate Chendo with an astute ball down the right, inside Sansom. He then collected the return after it had passed through a forest of legs in the English penalty-area and coolly shot past Shilton from eight yards.

But confident England barely had to break stride, scoring twice in the next quarter of an hour to set themselves up for a famous victory. Gary Lineker's first effort to count arrived in the 24th minute, after Bryan Robson had curled his shot against a post and Spanish goalkeeper Zubizarreta had been knocked backwards by the force of Glenn Hoddle's volley from the rebound. Hoddle then chipped the loose ball back over the scrambling Zubizarreta and Lineker headed home at the far post.

Viv Anderson, the England full-back who likes to get forward at set-pieces, nodded Hoddle's free-kick down into the path of Lineker four minutes later and the spring-heeled striker slid the ball in for his second goal. Lineker then completed his hat-trick two minutes after half-time as he bravely got his head to a dropping ball after Zubizarreta had deflected Peter Beardsley's deliberate shot into the air.

Lineker's fourth and last (in the 56th minute) was arguably the best of the night. Beardsley pushed an inviting pass along the edge of the area and Lineker took it in his stride before shooting left-footed across Zubizarreta and just inside the right-hand post. The man with the Midas touch had done it again, becoming the first player to score more than three in an England international since Malcolm MacDonald managed five against Cyprus at Wembley in 1975.

With more than half an hour of the match still to go and the Spanish rear-guard in some disarray, England must have been expecting a couple more goals at least. But it didn't turn out that way, as the home team salvaged some pride with a consolation goal that produced a final scoreline of 4–2 (an embarrassing defeat but not a humiliating one). Chris Woods, brought on to relieve Shilton in England's goal, saved impressively from Ramon before being beaten by the same player in the 76th minute.

Woods needn't have worried too much. In his next 12 England games, including substitute appearances, he conceded *one* goal.

Lineker's third goal flies into the Spanish net

Lineker's second goal gets past a full-back and the goalkeeper

SOCCER KNOWLEDGE

4

1

Who scored five goals in an Under-21 international against France in 1990?
A. Mark Robins
B. Lee Sharpe
C. Graeme Le Saux

2

Who is the top goal-scorer of all time for Oldham Athletic?
A. Andy Ritchie
B. Roger Palmer
C. Joe Royle

3

Who was the first player to win his first England cap under Graham Taylor?
A. Gary Pallister
B. Chris Woods
C. Ian Wright

4

Who is the youngest player ever to have represented England at Under-21 level?
A. Lee Chapman
B. Lee Sharpe
C. Lee Dixon

5

With which club did Mark Wright make his League debut in 1981?
A. Derby County
B. Southampton
C. Oxford United

6

Away from the game, what is the No.1 hobby of most footballers?
A. Golf
B. Fishing
C. Snooker

7

How many times did Bobby Charlton captain England?
A. 60
B. 20
C. 3

8

For which team did Gary Lineker score an FA Cup Final goal in 1986?
A. Leicester City
B. Everton
C. Tottenham Hotspur

9

Trevor Francis has been playing first team football since he was 16 years old. He was called 'Superboy' at his first club – which?
A. Manchester City
B. Aston Villa
C. Birmingham City

10

Jürgen Klinsmann is an international player for which country?
A. Wales
B. Germany
C. Austria

Mark Wright and John Barnes in action against Holland, June 1990

11

What colour shirts do Brazil wear if their first choice clashes with the opposition?
A. Blue
B. Red
C. Yellow

12

Who coached the West German team to World Cup success in 1990?
A. Sepp Maier
B. Bertie Vogts
C. Franz Beckenbauer

13

David Seaman became the most expensive goalkeeper in the world when he left which club to join Arsenal for £1.2m in 1990?
A. QPR
B. WBA
C. Derby County

14

Apart from the two reserve goalkeepers, only one player in England's World Cup squad did not see any action. Who was he?
A. Gary Stevens
B. Paul Parker
C. Steve Hodge

15

With which club did Gary Lineker form a striking partnership with Alan Smith?
A. Leicester City
B. Arsenal
C. Northampton Town

16

Who was the top goal-scorer in the 1990 World Cup with six goals?
A. Ruud Gullit
B. Toto Schillaci
C. Roberto Baggio

17

Whose ground have Bristol Rovers been using for several seasons?
A. Bath City
B. Bristol City
C. Portsmouth

18

Who was England's goalkeeper when they won the World Cup in 1966?
A. Gordon Banks
B. Peter Shilton
C. Phil Parkes

19

Which team play at Elland Road?
A. Everton
B. Leeds United
C. Aldershot

David Seaman in the Friendly against Cameroon, February 1991

20

Which team were once called St Domingo?
A. Everton
B. Southampton
C. Fulham

21

Which player has scored the most hat-tricks in League football? (The record is 37.)
A. Jimmy Greaves
B. 'Dixie' Dean
C. Ian Rush

22

Who finished in third place in the 1990 World Cup Finals?
A. Argentina
B. England
C. Italy

23

Which team play at The Dell?
A. Southampton
B. Northampton Town
C. West Ham United

24

Which player has scored the most League goals in Wimbledon's history?
A. John Fashanu
B. Hans Segers
C. Alan Cork

25

What country would you be in if you were watching Nancy play Metz?
A. France
B. USA
C. Spain

Answers on page 61

England Team Doctor

International games are no holiday for at least one member of the team – the England doctor.

Dr John Crane – the England team doctor

Why does a team need a doctor? Well, professional footballers, apart from being very expensive, are finely-tuned athletes. When they play a match for their country they need to be able to run hard for 90 minutes (and sometimes, as we saw in the World Cup, for 120 minutes). They have to perform their skills as well at the end of a match as at the beginning, to be able to take knocks without getting injured, to stay sharp-witted – and then to recover quickly from all that effort in time for the next game. Treating injuries is only part of this. Somebody has to make sure that the players are properly fed, that they get enough sleep, have the right treatment if they're ill and that they have somebody to talk to if they have any personal problems. That person is Dr John Crane, the England team doctor.

John studied medicine at Liverpool University and qualified as a doctor in 1955. Three years later he moved to London and became a General Practitioner. He always had a great interest in sport and worked in the Sports Clinic at Guys Hospital for ten years. In 1970 he became one of the team doctors at Arsenal FC and has remained so ever since.

During the '70s Dr Crane acted as team doctor at several England Youth Internationals and was promoted to Dave Sexton's Under-21 team in 1977. He looked after the Under-21s when they won the UEFA Championship in 1982 and 1984. Then in 1986 came the big step-up. During the Mexico World Cup the England seniors' doctor, Vernon Edwards, was taken ill and had to go into hospital in Monterrey. John Crane was sent for and, when Dr Edwards was advised to take life a little more easily, he was offered the position full-time.

So what does the team doctor do? Let John Crane take you through a typical match in his own words.

Each match starts for me with a letter from the FA telling me where we shall be staying and when to report. My first move is to get in touch with the manager of the hotel to arrange the meals. I don't think the players eat enough. I know the manager and the lads think I go on a bit about food, but the human body is an engine, and when you're going to ask that engine to work flat out for 90 minutes, you need to make sure it gets enough of the right fuel! I try to work out an interesting and balanced diet. The important thing is that the players get enough carbohydrates down them in the 24 hours leading up to the game. That means pasta, potatoes, bread, chocolate, ice cream and my own personal favourite, rice pudding! For the last meal before a match I think it's best to let players have what they feel happy with. Some like baked beans, others steaks, some spaghetti. I rather like them to have a Mars bar or ice cream as well.

When the team meets, I try to see every player as quickly as possible and find out if he has any knocks or minor illnesses. Fred Street and Norman Medhurst get down to treating any injuries as soon as they can, because we don't have long to get the lads fit. If a player is obviously not going to make it in time for the game, we like to get him home as soon as possible. If we have an injury during training, I have to know where I am going to take the player if he needs an x-ray or has to be taken into hospital. This is one of the first jobs I have to do on arrival abroad for a match. Most countries have good facilities for sports injuries, but some I need to go and see for myself, just to be sure.

It isn't only the players, of course. I have to look after the other members of the England party too. At one time during the last World Cup I had the Chairman of the International Committee, the England Manager and several journalists on the 'injured' list, as well as various players. Sometimes when we are abroad, I know the players think I nag about them not eating outside the hotel. I don't like ice in drinks or uncooked food. As far as I'm concerned, it's better to be safe than sorry. A bad tummy can put a player out of a big match just as surely as a twisted ankle. I'm happy to say that we went right through the 1986 and 1990 World Cups without losing one player's services through careless eating.

When the game is over and I am back home, I send reports to the clubs about their players' fitness, as it's very important for them to know what treatment the players have been having and whether there have been any injuries. Then I have to face all my partners at the surgery who tell me how hard they've been working while I've been away on holiday!

Ouch! Des Walker received on-the-spot treatment to his right ankle, injured in the match against Belgium, June 1990

England Challenge Cup

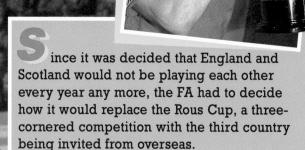

S ince it was decided that England and Scotland would not be playing each other every year any more, the FA had to decide how it would replace the Rous Cup, a three-cornered competition with the third country being invited from overseas.

The answer was to invite two of the world's top countries and to let them play the third game in the tournament against each other. The planning for these games began as early as the 1990 World Cup finals, when the USSR and finalists, Argentina, agreed to come to England the following summer.

*Above right: England's captain Gary Lineker with the England Challenge Cup
Above: David Platt with the USSR's Alexander Mostovoi*

Wembley Stadium is the ground for all England's matches so it was certain that the games against Argentina and USSR would be played there, but the match between USSR and Argentina gave the FA the chance to put a full international on another ground for the first time since the 1966 World Cup finals. After careful consideration, Manchester United's Old Trafford ground was picked.

The competition got under way with England v USSR at Wembley on 21 May 1991. The visitors were the first into their stride and shocked England with an early goal, deflected past Chris Woods in the England goal by his team-mate Mark Wright, making his first appearance as England captain. England looked shaky for a time as the Soviets played some neat football, but the home side's more direct play was rewarded before half-time with a first international goal from Alan Smith and a penalty by David Platt after the player himself had been brought down in the area. The USSR team continued to enjoy

a lot of possession without threatening the England defence, but it was David Platt again who wrapped up the win with a third goal just before the end.

On 23 May, Argentina and the USSR played a very competitive match at Old Trafford. The USSR missed a first-half penalty, before Ruggeri gave the South Americans a lead right on the interval with a far-post header. The Soviets came back strongly in the second half and equalised with a free-kick from Kolyvanov.

That left the England v Argentina match on 25 May as the decider. England started brightly with an opening goal from ace striker Gary Lineker, his 40th for England. Early in the second half, David Platt headed in his third of the tournament and England looked to be coasting. Argentina had other ideas and came back with great headed goals from Garcia and Franco. That left the home team with a few anxious moments, but they held on for the draw that gave them the handsome England Challenge Cup for 1991.

	P	W	D	L	F	A	Pts
England	2	1	1	0	5	3	3
Argentina	2	0	2	0	3	3	2
USSR	2	0	1	1	2	4	1

Gary Lineker scores England's first goal against Argentina

England Travel Club

Thinking of going abroad to see England play? Then why not join the England Travel Club – it has a lot to offer.

A few of the many dedicated England fans who travel the world to watch the national team

The England Travel Club was introduced in 1989 to help fans who wanted to visit England matches abroad but who did not want to be treated like hooligans. For a long time, The Football Association had been obliged to say to supporters that it would be better if they didn't go to see England play abroad. This was not because it was thought that they would be likely to cause trouble, but because there was a tiny number of so-called fans who, over a long period of time, had made the rest of the world think that whenever England came to play there was likely to be trouble.

The FA decided that it would not obtain any tickets for games abroad and it tried to get as much publicity as possible to try to persuade people not to travel. As a result, the number of supporters who went abroad for England games became less and less. The trouble that was caused also became less and the people who had no interest in the football, but only went to see what a nuisance they could make of themselves, became easier to spot and to control.

The decision to set up a Travel Club was made after the 1988 European Championship, when the FA handled tickets for the England supporters. The FA was very pleased with the behaviour of those who had had tickets from it. There were some very worrying newspaper and television reports about the English fans in general. But much of this was untrue and the FA was satisfied that the supporters who had been given official tickets had stayed out of trouble. Nevertheless, it was clear that it was not going to be possible to stop fans from travelling in large numbers to the big tournaments in Europe. The Football Association needed to set up a system not only to control the allocation of tickets, but also to offer the supporters a chance to join something that would show the people abroad that they were not going to cause any trouble.

you wanted just to make sure that you could get into games. The FA realised that a lot of supporters would not be able to afford the higher priced tickets and let the fans have them at the lower prices. A lot of supporters travelled without joining the Travel Club, but they were allowed to join, provided they agreed to accept the same standards of behaviour as those people who had become members before the World Cup. Altogether, another 2000 were enrolled while in Italy.

Why should anyone join the Travel Club? Well, first of all, the members get the first chance to buy tickets for England matches at home and abroad. This has meant that Travel Club members have been able to get tickets for the World Cup finals and they will be first in line for the European Championship and the next World Cup in America. They also have the chance to get tickets for big Wembley matches, such as England against Brazil or the Republic of Ireland.

Members get a regular newsletter from the FA, in which they are given details of matches, news from the England team and the chance to buy England souvenirs at discount prices. In the future, The Football Association will be developing the Travel Club so that it can offer a travel service to its members alongside the ticket offers.

Many of the Travel Club members are youngsters and it is the wish of the FA that more and more people should come to see England play at home and away as a family. The Family Enclosure at Wembley gives mums and dads the chance to take their children to an international at half price, to see the match in safety and comfort and to go home with a souvenir with the compliments of the FA and the Family Enclosure sponsors, BBC Radio 1.

Young or old, if you want to join the Travel Club, write to:

The England Travel Club
The Football Association
16 Lancaster Gate
London
W2 3LW

It was agreed that The Football Association would take as many tickets as it could get for England's matches in the World Cup and would sell these only to members of the newly-formed Travel Club. In the months leading up to the 1990 World Cup nearly 5000 people joined. The FA set up an office in each of the towns in which England played and made sure that the Travel Club members got the tickets they had asked for. In fact, the FA lost a lot of money in the process, because the system of ticket sales in Italy meant that you often had to buy tickets at a higher price than

Junior England Soccer Club

Have you joined The Juniors yet?

The Football Association has just launched a club that is for youngsters interested in football. Does that sound like you?

The new club's full name is The FA England Junior Soccer Club, but at the FA's London headquarters we call it 'The Juniors'. You don't need to be a great player to join, in fact you don't have to be a player at all...you just need to be soccer mad!

All members receive a full-colour, glossy 24 page quarterly magazine jam-packed with football fun, action shots, soccer skill tips from star players, coaching by top FA coaches, news updates, special offers and big prize competitions. Look out also for our super-action comic strip, where you will meet a brand new soccer hero.

Your starter pack will contain the first issue of your magazine, your club badge, membership card, certificate and a full colour poster of the England squad.

For further details about The Juniors, write to:

Club World Ltd
The Juniors
Covden House
7a Langley Street
London
WC2H 9JA

Three young England fans at the World Cup finals in Italy

England Ball-boys

For the nine ball-boys at an England international at Wembley it must be a dream come true. But how did they become ball-boys in the first place?

The ball-boys for England internationals at Wembley are provided by County Football Associations, with the counties themselves chosen by ballot at a meeting of the FA's Match and Grounds Committee. That means that there is a kind of rota system whereby every county has an opportunity to nominate some of its young footballers to act as ball-boys on important Wembley nights for Graham Taylor's England team.

Nine boys are needed for ball-boy duties and they are normally brought to Wembley Stadium in a coach, accompanied by one or two County FA members. They are expected to arrive 3 to $3\frac{1}{2}$ hours before kick-off and they have to report to Mike Appleby, the FA official in charge of them, at the entrance to the players' tunnel. They are taken to their changing room and, on the way, given an opportunity to look around the England team's dressing room. The players' shirts will already be hanging on pegs and all the equipment will be laid out by England physiotherapists Fred Street and Norman Medhurst. There will be a chance of a quick chat with Fred and Norman. '*Is Gazza going to be fit?*' they all want to know.

The boys are then allocated their on-field positions: three lots of two boys for the two sides and the far end, and one group of three boys for the tunnel end. Mike Appleby will walk them around the pitch and explain how they must keep on the move and not stand too close to the fence while the match is in progress – otherwise supporters will complain that they can't see the action!

At half-time and full-time the ball-boys gather behind the goal at the tunnel end before

This is to Certify

that

_____

has been a

BALLBOY

at Wembley Stadium

on the occasion of

_____

on _____

Chief Executive

All ball-boys at England internationals receive this special certificate

following the teams back to the dressing room area. The boys will be wearing equipment provided by the FA: sky blue shirts, shorts and socks and blue tracksuits (or wetsuits). Sandwiches and a drink are provided as they get changed before the game and they have to be ready to go out about half-an-hour prior to kick-off. Before they take up their positions a group photograph will be taken of them on the pitch and a copy of that, plus a certificate, will act as mementoes of a very special day. '*I threw the ball to Lineker and seconds later the ball was in the net,*' is how one lucky ball-boy remembered his big match!

Hat-trick Heroes

The three goals scored by Geoff Hurst in the 1966 World Cup Final have gone down in soccer history. But he is not the only player to have achieved this feat in games for England...

Geoff Hurst playing in the Charity Friendly against West Germany, July 1985. This was a 'replay' of the 1966 match. England won 6–4

The term 'hat-trick', which is used in soccer to denote three consecutive goals for a team scored by the same player, originates from cricket. It dates back to the days when a bowler was presented with a new hat by his club whenever he succeeded in taking three wickets with three balls.

Strictly speaking, it is not correct to credit a player with a hat-trick in soccer if his sequence of three goals is broken by a goal from another player for the same side. However, when players or supporters talk about a player scoring a hat-trick, they usually mean that he (or she) has netted three times in the same game. That, in fact, is all a player needs to have done if he wants to claim the match ball!

The first England players to manage three goals or more in an international match were Oliver Vaughton and Arthur Brown, scorers of five and four respectively against Ireland, in Belfast, on 18 February 1882. England won 13–0, and it still remains the team's largest margin of victory in an official international.

There were 23 hat-tricks before World War I, including the first on the continent when Vivian Woodward got four goals and Frank Bradshaw three as England won 11–1 in Austria. There were ten hat-tricks between the wars and there have been 38 since 1945. Forty-eight *different* players have registered hat-tricks for England since records began – Gary Lineker being the latest in the 1991 international against Malaysia. The most famous 'hat-trick hero' has undoubtedly been Geoff Hurst, whose three goals helped England to World Cup victory in 1966.

Lineker, with five hat-tricks (scored against Turkey in 1985, Poland in 1986, Spain and Turkey in 1987, and Malaysia in 1991), has now overtaken two illustrious predecessors in Vivian Woodward and Bobby Charlton, who can claim four each. Jimmy Greaves, goal poacher supreme, holds the record with six England hat-tricks scored between 1960 and 1966. Greaves was a member of the most prolific England team of modern times – one which scored no fewer than 40 goals in six matches during the free-scoring 1960–61 season.

England's 'Hat-trick heroes'

Date	Opponents	Venue	Result	Scorer
18.2.1882	Ireland	Belfast	13–0	Vaughton 5, A. Brown 4
3.2.1883	Wales	Oval	5–0	Mitchell 3
25.2.1884	Ireland	Belfast	8–1	Cursham 3
13.3.1886	Ireland	Belfast	6–1	Spilsbury 4
5.2.1887	Ireland	Sheffield	7–0	Lindley 3
31.3.1888	Ireland	Belfast	5–1	Allen 3
2.3.1889	ireland	Everton	6–1	Yates 3
15.3.1890	Ireland	Belfast	9–1	Geary 3
25.2.1893	Ireland	Birmingham	6–1	Gilliat 3
12.3.1894	Wales	Wrexham	5–1	Veitch 3
16.3.1896	Wales	Cardiff	9–1	Bloomer 5
20.2.1897	Ireland	Nottingham	6–0	Wheldon 3
18.2.1899	Ireland	Sunderland	13–2	G. Smith 4, Settle 3
18.3.1901	Wales	Newcastle	6–0	Bloomer 4
16.3.1908	Wales	Wrexham	7–1	Woodward 3
8.6.1908	Austria	Vienna	11–1	Woodward 4, Bradshaw 3
10.6.1908	Hungary	Budapest	7–0	Hilsdon 4
31.5.1909	Hungary	Budapest	8–2	Woodward 4
1.6.1909	Austria	Vienna	8–1	Woodward 3
10.2.1912	Ireland	Dublin	6–1	Fleming 3
24.5.1926	Belgium	Antwerp	5–3	Osborne 3
11.5.1927	Belgium	Brussels	9–1	Dean 3
21.5.1927	Luxembourg	Luxembourg	5–2	Dean 3
11.5.1929	Belgium	Brussels	5–1	Camsell 4
20.11.1929	Wales	Chelsea	6–0	Camsell 3
2.12.1936	Hungary	Arsenal	6–2	Drake 3
17.5.1937	Sweden	Stockholm	4–0	Steele 3
23.10.1937	Ireland	Belfast	5–1	Mills 3
1.12.1937	Czechoslovakia	Tottenham	5–4	Matthews 3
16.11.1938	Ireland	Manchester	7–0	Hall 5
28.9.1946	Ireland	Belfast	7–2	Mannion 3
27.11.1946	Holland	Huddersfield	8–2	Lawton 4
25.5.1947	Portugal	Lisbon	10–0	Mortensen 4, Lawton 4
19.11.1947	Sweden	Arsenal	4–2	Mortensen 3
9.10.1948	Ireland	Belfast	6–2	Mortensen 3
15.10.1949	Wales	Cardiff	4–1	Milburn 3
16.11.1949	Ireland	Manchester	9–2	Rowley 4
14.5.1950	Portugal	Lisbon	5–3	Finney 4
10.11.1954	Wales	Wembley	3–2	Bentley 3
2.4.1955	Scotland	Wembley	7–2	Wilshaw 4
5.12.1956	Denmark	Wolverhampton	5–2	Taylor 3
8.5.1957	Eire	Wembley	5–1	Taylor 3
22.10.1958	USSR	Wembley	5–0	Haynes 3
28.5.1959	USA	Los Angeles	8–1	Charlton 3
19.10.1960	Luxembourg	Luxembourg	9–0	Greaves 3, Charlton 3
15.4.1961	Scotland	Wembley	9–3	Greaves 3
10.5.1961	Mexico	Wembley	8–0	Charlton 3
20.5.1962	Peru	Lima	4–0	Greaves 3
5.6.1963	Switzerland	Basle	8–1	Charlton 3
20.11.1963	Ireland	Wembley	8–3	Greaves 4, Paine 3
17.5.1964	Portugal	Lisbon	4–3	Byrne 3
27.5.1964	USA	New York	10–0	Hunt 4, Pickering 3
3.10.1964	Ireland	Belfast	4–3	Greaves 3
29.6.1966	Norway	Oslo	6–1	Greaves 4
30.7.1966	West Germany	Wembley	4–2	Hurst 3
12.3.1969	France	Wembley	5–0	Hurst 3
16.4.1975	Cyprus	Wembley	5–0	MacDonald 5
15.12.1982	Luxembourg	Wembley	9–0	Blissett 3
14.11.1984	Turkey	Istanbul	8–0	Robson 3
16.10.1985	Turkey	Wembley	5–0	Lineker 3
11.6.1986	Poland	Monterrey	3–0	Lineker 3
18.2.1987	Spain	Madrid	4–2	Lineker 4
14.10.1987	Turkey	Wembley	8–0	Lineker 3
12.6.1991	Malaysia	Kuala Lumpur	4–2	Lineker 4

Top: Geoff Hurst
Middle: Jimmy Greaves
Bottom: Gary Lineker

ENGLAND
Soccer Knowledge
COMPETITION

This is your big chance to see England in a full international at Wembley! We have three pairs of tickets to give away for the match with France on Wednesday, 19 February 1992.

Here's what you have to do:

Look at Bob Thomas's three great action photos on these two pages. Then answer these three questions:

1 *Bryan Robson scores one of England's four goals against Yugoslavia in 1987. In which city was this match played?*

2 *Neil Webb is challenged by two Scottish defenders at Wembley. In which competition was this particular match?*

3 *Gary Lineker gets the better of Colombian defender Perea. How many times have Colombia visited Wembley?*

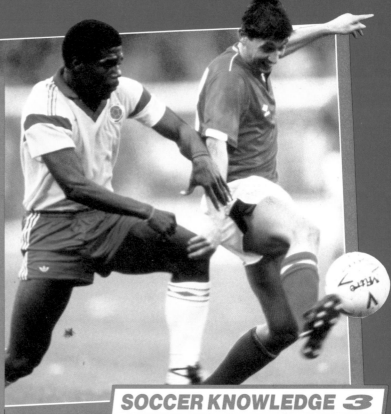

SOCCER KNOWLEDGE 3

Complete the entry form below and send it to the address shown before 3 February 1992. Send a photocopy if you don't want to cut the page.

The readers sending the first three correct entries to be drawn on 3 February 1992 will each win a pair of tickets for the England v France international at Wembley on 19 February 1992.

ENGLAND *SOCCER KNOWLEDGE* COMPETITION

Write your answers in the spaces provided

SOCCER KNOWLEDGE 1

Name of city:

. . . .

SOCCER KNOWLEDGE 2

Name of competition:

. . . .

SOCCER KNOWLEDGE 3

Number of visits:

. . . .

Your name . . . .

Age . . . .

Address . . . .

. . . .

. . . .

All entry forms should be returned to the following address:

England Soccer Knowledge Competition
Editorial Department
World International Publishing Limited
P.O. Box 111 Great Ducie Street
Manchester M60 3BL

Don't forget! *The closing date is 3 February 1992*

Diary
of Football Events 1992

JANUARY

Sat 4   FA Challenge Cup
         3rd Round
Wed 8   Rumbelows Cup 5th
         Round
Sat 25   FA Challenge Cup
         4th Round

FEBRUARY

Wed 12   Rumbelows Cup
         Semi-Final (1st Leg)
Sat 15   FA Challenge Cup
         5th Round
Wed 19   England v France
         (Friendly)

The world watches. Photographers at an international match with the teams on the pitch as the national anthems are played

MARCH

Wed 4   Rumbelows Cup
         Semi-Final (2nd Leg)
Wed 4   European Champion
         Clubs' Cup 3rd Round
         (1st Leg)
Wed 4   European Cup
         Winners' Cup 3rd
         Round (1st Leg)
Wed 4   UEFA Cup 4th Round
         (1st Leg)
Sat 7   FA Challenge Cup
         6th Round
Wed 18   European Champion
         Clubs' Cup 3rd Round
         (2nd Leg)
Wed 18   European Cup
         Winners' Cup 3rd
         Round (2nd Leg)
Wed 18   UEFA Cup 4th
         Round (2nd Leg)
Wed 25   Czechoslovakia v
         England (Friendly)

APRIL

Wed 1   European Champion
         Clubs' Cup Semi-Final
         (1st Leg)
Wed 1   European Cup
         Winners' Cup
         Semi-Final (1st Leg)

Wed 1   UEFA Cup Semi-Final
         (1st Leg)
Sun 5   FA Challenge Cup
         Semi-Final
Sun 12   Rumbelows Cup Final
Wed 15   European Champion
         Clubs' Cup Semi-Final
         (2nd Leg)
Wed 15   European Cup
         Winners' Cup Semi-
         Final (2nd Leg)
Wed 15   UEFA Cup Semi-Final
         (2nd Leg)
Wed 29   USSR v England
         (Friendly)
Wed 29   UEFA Cup Final (1st
         Leg)

MAY

Wed 6   European Cup
         Winners' Cup Final
Sat 9   FA Challenge Cup
         Final
Tue 12   International Date
Wed 13   UEFA Cup Final (2nd
         Leg)
Thu 14   FA Challenge Cup
         Final Possible Replay
Fri 15   International Date
Sun 17   International Date
Wed 20   European Champion
         Clubs' Cup Final

JUNE

Wed 3   Finland v England
         (Friendly)
Wed 10   European
         Championship Finals
         in Sweden (end 26th)

Answers

SOCCER KNOWLEDGE 1

1	Bobby Robson	14	Ciao
2	Leicester City v Hull City	15	Graham Kelly
		16	No
3	No, it's a competition for top non-league sides only	17	Notts County, formed in 1862
4	17	18	Holland
5	Berwick Rangers	19	Bobby Moore (108 caps)
6	Brentford		
7	PSV Eindhoven	20	Mitre
8	Royal	21	Italy, in July 1990
9	European Cup Winners' Cup	22	No, but corner flags are in all matches
10	Blackpool	23	True, (before he joined Newcastle)
11	Peter Shilton		
12	Colchester United v Leyton Orient	24	No
		25	To pass the ball through an opponent's legs
13	Yes, briefly in 1973–74		

Des Walker and West Germany's Rudi Voeller, July 1990

SOCCER KNOWLEDGE 2

1	B	6	C	11	A	16	C	21	A
2	C	7	B	12	A	17	B	22	B
3	B	8	A	13	A	18	A	23	A
4	B	9	C	14	B	19	C	24	C
5	B	10	B	15	C	20	B	25	C

SOCCER KNOWLEDGE 3

1	Preston North End	13	The senior linesman
2	Jack Charlton	14	Yes, it is a stipulation in the Laws of the Game
3	Coventry City		
4	The Football Association Challenge Cup Competition		
		15	Gary Lineker, 4 goals
		16	Leicester City
		17	True
5	None, the rule allowing two was abolished in 1990	18	France
		19	Derby County
		20	True
6	Spain	21	Crystal Palace
7	They are the current Italian League Champions	22	Everton, founded in 1878 (Liverpool 1892)
		23	Spurs, founded in 1882 (Arsenal 1886)
8	Cameroon		
9	Because the Pilgrim Fathers set sail for America from Plymouth	24	Manchester United, founded in 1878 (Manchester City 1887)
10	Celtic and Liverpool	25	The club's founder was impressed with the shirts worn by Notts County nearly 100 years ago
11	Czechoslovakia		
12	Queens Park Rangers have had 12 different homes		

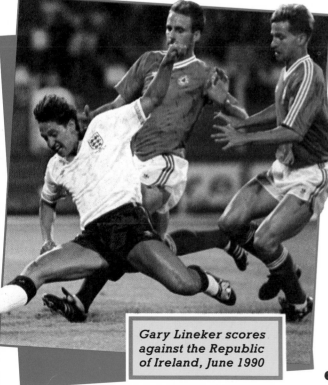

Gary Lineker scores against the Republic of Ireland, June 1990

SOCCER KNOWLEDGE 4

1	A	6	A	11	A	16	B	21	B
2	B	7	C	12	C	17	A	22	C
3	C	8	B	13	A	18	A	23	A
4	B	9	C	14	C	19	B	24	C
5	C	10	B	15	A	20	A	25	A

England's Gary Lineker beats Republic of Ireland's Pat Bonner to score in the World Cup finals, June 1990